AMERICAN
INDIVIDUALISM

RELATED WRITINGS OF HERBERT HOOVER

The Challenge to Liberty (1934)

The Memoirs of Herbert Hoover
(Three volumes, 1951–1952)

Addresses Upon the American Road
(Eight volumes, 1938–1961)

An American Epic
(Four volumes, 1959–1964)

*Freedom Betrayed: Herbert Hoover's Secret History
of the Second World War and Its Aftermath*
(Hoover Institution Press, 2011)

*The Crusade Years, 1933–1955: Herbert Hoover's
Lost Memoir of the New Deal Era and Its Aftermath*
(Hoover Institution Press, 2013)

AMERICAN INDIVIDUALISM

by

HERBERT HOOVER

With an Introduction by
George H. Nash

HOOVER INSTITUTION PRESS
Stanford University | Stanford, California

www.hoover.org

Hoover Institution Press Publication No. 675

Hoover Institution Leland Stanford Junior University, Stanford, California 94305-6003

American Individualism was first published in 1922 by Doubleday, Page & Company.
Introduction © 2016 by George H. Nash. Adapted from the introduction to *American Individualism, 1933/The Challenge to Liberty, 1934*, © 1989 by The Hoover Presidential Foundation.

First printing 2016

23 22 21 20 19 18 17   10 9 8 7 6 5 4 3 2

Manufactured in the United States of America

The paper used in this publication meets the minimum requirements of the American National Standard for Information Sciences—Permanence of Paper for Printed Library Materials, ANSI/NISO Z39.48-1992. ∞

Cataloging-in-Publication Data is available from the Library of Congress.
ISBN-13: 978-0-8179-2015-9 (paper : alk. paper)
ISBN-13: 978-0-8179-2016-6 (epub)
ISBN-13: 978-0-8179-2017-3 (mobi)
ISBN-13: 978-0-8179-2018-0 (PDF)

CONTENTS

INTRODUCTION

I

On September 13, 1919, Herbert Hoover returned to the United States a troubled man. Ten months before, at the conclusion of the First World War, he had sailed to Europe at President Woodrow Wilson's request to administer food relief on a continent careening toward catastrophe. The once mighty German and Austro-Hungarian empires—America's enemies in the war—lay shattered. Across

Introduction © 2016 by George H. Nash. Adapted from the introduction to *American Individualism, 1922/The Challenge to Liberty, 1934*, © 1989 by The Hoover Presidential Foundation.

vast stretches of Europe, as 1919 began, famine, disease, and bloody revolution threatened to sunder a civilization already deeply wounded by "the war to end all war."

As Wilson and the Allied leaders of Great Britain, France, and Italy struggled to draft a peace treaty in Paris, Hoover and his American Relief Administration delivered food to millions of people, reorganized the transportation and communications networks of nations prostrate from conflict, and helped check the advance of communist revolution from the East. Thanks in considerable measure to the Herculean efforts of Hoover and his associates, perhaps one-third of the population of postwar Europe was saved from starvation and death.

As Hoover journeyed home to America, his personal reputation was at its zenith. Five years earlier, as a respected American mining engineer living in London, he had organized a private relief agency that delivered and distributed food to the entire civilian population of Belgium (more than 7 million people) for the duration of the war. It was a voluntary, philanthropic effort without precedent in human history, and it made him an international hero. Now, from Finland to Armenia, from the streets of Vienna to the plains of eastern Poland, his name and that of the American Relief Administration were hailed for their humanitarian achievements. Tens of millions of people owed their lives to his exertions. In America he was lauded as "the Napoleon of Mercy." In Great Britain, John Maynard Keynes called him "the only man who emerged from the ordeal of Paris with an enhanced reputation."[1]

Yet that autumn Hoover was not content. For several months he had pleaded with the Allied leaders in Paris to lift their blockade of the defeated German enemy and allow the healing currents of peaceful exchange to flow. Only after a long, wearisome struggle did he attain this objective. Every day at the peace conference he had witnessed a dispiriting display of national rivalry, vengefulness, and greed. He had observed, too, the sometimes violent attempts of reformers and radicals to construct a new social order on the principles of Marxist socialism. It was a time, he said, of "stupendous social ferment and revolution."[2]

Hoover returned to his native land and (he soon told friends) with "two convictions . . . dominant in my mind." The first was that the ideology of socialism, as tested before his eyes in Europe, was a catastrophic failure. Socialism's fundamental premises—that the "impulse of altruism" could alone maintain productivity and that bureaucracy at the top could determine the most productive roles for each individual—said Hoover, were false. Only the "primary school of competition," Hoover countered, could do that. Oblivious to this truth and to the fundamental human impulse of self-interest, socialism had "wrecked itself on the rock of production." It was unable to motivate men and women to produce sufficient goods for the needs of society. Without increased productivity and the resultant plenty, neither social harmony nor an improved standard of living for the masses would occur. To Hoover the economic demoralization of Europe in 1919, with its attendant suffering, was the direct result of the bankruptcy of socialism.[3]

Hoover's second conviction was also firmly held. More than ever before he sensed the "enormous distance" that America had traveled from Europe during 150 years of nationhood.[4] To Hoover it now seemed that "irreconcilable conflicts" in ideals and experience separated the Old World from the New.[5] The New World, he came to believe, was remote from the imperialism, fanatic ideologies, "age-old hates," racial antipathies, dictatorships, power politics, and class stratifications of Europe. What the engineer-humanitarian had witnessed at the Paris peace conference, he came to believe, was something far more profound than "the intrigues of diplomacy or the foibles of European statesmen." It was "the collision of civilizations that had grown three hundred years apart."[6]

These sentiments of Hoover's to some extent predated the trauma of 1919. Before the outbreak of the Great War, he had been an extraordinarily successful international mining engineer and financier. Born in Iowa in 1874 and orphaned before he was ten, by the time he was forty he had spent most of his adulthood outside the United States, in environments as various as the goldfields of the Australian outback, the coal mines of northern China, the rain forests of Burma, and the corporate boardrooms of London. He had traversed the Trans-Siberian Railway and journeyed around the world several times. This early and prolonged exposure to foreign civilizations led Hoover to notice and reflect on the remarkable contrasts in politics, economics, and philosophy of life between other societies and his own. Why, he wondered, was America so different? Why was America unique?

That America *was* different, he had no doubt. "Every homecoming" to his native shores, he later wrote, "was an inspiration." In America he found "a greater kindliness, a greater neighborliness, a greater sense of individual responsibility, a lesser poverty, a greater comfort and security of our people, a wider spread of education, a wider diffusion of the finer arts and appreciation of them, a greater freedom of spirit, a wider opportunity for our children, and higher hopes of the future, than in any other country in the world."[7] This was how he had felt after his numerous engineering journeys before 1914. It was how he felt in September 1919 as he boarded a ship in Europe and headed home.

Yet Hoover was by no means complacent. The disorders and disorientation gripping Europe had cast a pall over the New World as well as the Old. During 1919 the United States experienced bitter and frightening upheavals: a massive strike in the steel industry, a police strike and mob violence in Boston, a general strike in Seattle, race riots in twenty towns and cities, the lynching of seventy-six African Americans, the founding of the Communist Party, and the attempted assassination by bombing of several leading public officials.

Coming back to America from Europe, Hoover sensed that his beloved homeland was vulnerable to the afflictions he had just witnessed abroad. To an assembly of American mining engineers he declared early in 1920: "We face a Europe still at war; still amid social revolutions; some of its peoples still slacking on production; millions starving; and therefore the safety of its civilization is still hanging by a slender thread. Every wind that blows carries to our shores an infection of social disease from this great ferment; every convulsion there has an economic reaction upon our own people."[8] Hoover implored his fellow citizens not to turn their country into "a laboratory for experiment in foreign social diseases."[9] Instead he contended that a "definite American substitute is needed for these disintegrating theories of Europe"—a substitute grounded in "our national instincts" and "the normal development of our national institutions."[10]

In numerous speeches and articles in 1919–20 Hoover began to define this American "substitute." The foundation of America's distinctive social philosophy, he asserted, was the principle of equality of opportunity: the idea that no one should be "handicapped in securing that particular niche in the community to which his abilities and character entitle him." Unlike Europe, where oppressive class barriers had generated misery and discontent, the American social system was based on "the negation of class." A society, said Hoover, in which there is "a constant flux of individuals in the community, upon the basis of ability and character, is a moving virile mass."[11] Such a society was the United States of America.

Hoover was neither a nativist nor a standpatter. Time and again in those turbulent months, he insisted that America's ideals comported with neither radicalism nor reaction. To Hoover the convulsions in Europe were an understandable response to long-festering social injustice, and, although the socialist panacea was a ghastly error, the alternative was not the status quo antebellum. "We shall never remedy justifiable discontent," he asserted, "until we eradicate the misery which the ruthlessness of individualism has imposed upon a minority."[12] According to Hoover the solution to the problems of productivity and a "better division of the products of industry" lay not with the extremists of the Right or Left but with what he called "the liberal world of moderate men, working upon the safe foundations of experience."[13]

This, in 1920, was where Hoover perceived himself to be. A Bull Moose supporter of Theodore Roosevelt in 1912, a member of Woodrow Wilson's war cabinet during the recent conflict, and a self-styled "independent Progressive" as 1920 began, Hoover publicly identified himself with the Republican Party early in the year and unsuccessfully sought its presidential nomination. A few months later, President-elect Warren Harding appointed him secretary of commerce.

On March 4, 1921, the humanitarian-turned-technocrat entered Harding's cabinet and plunged with zeal into the task of reconstruction from the most terrible war the world had ever known. In short order Hoover became one of the three or four most influential men in American public life. It was said of him that he was secretary of commerce and undersecretary of every other department. But even as he applied his extraordinary energies to a formidable array of practical problems, the old questions continued to haunt him: How could America avoid the follies of war-ravaged Europe? How could the

American system as he understood it be strengthened in an age of revolution? Why was America so different? Why was America unique?

In late 1921 the secretary of commerce decided to distill from his experiences a coherent understanding of the American experiment he cherished. The result was the book *American Individualism*. Its genesis was an undelivered convocation address at an American university that autumn. Encouraged by his friend the journalist Mark Sullivan, Hoover decided to publish his manuscript. In the spring of 1922 it appeared as an article titled "American Individualism" in the magazine *World's Work*.[14] Late in the year, in a somewhat revised form, the essay was published as a book.

Hoover's volume—just seventy-two pages long—represented the crystallization of the attitudes and perceptions mentioned earlier. According to Hoover, the revolutionary upheavals of the recent Great War and its aftermath had produced a world in ferment. In this cauldron several "social philosophies"—among them communism, socialism, syndicalism, capitalism, and autocracy—were competing for the minds of people. To Hoover, who had seen the vicious results that emanate from a blending of "bestial instincts" with idealistic humanitarian jargon, the need for a definition of the American alternative was urgent. He labeled this alternative "American individualism."

By this term he did not mean unfettered, old-fashioned laissez-faire. As an accomplished engineer and businessman worth more than a million dollars by 1914, Hoover prized individual initiative—it was one of the character traits he most admired—and was anxious that it be stimulated and rewarded. Progress, he declared, "is almost solely dependent" on the few "creative minds" who "create or who carry discoveries to widespread application." But too much individualism—"individualism run riot"—could lead, in his view, to injustice and even tyranny in the form of the domination of government and business by the powerful.

The "values of individualism," Hoover argued, must therefore be "tempered"—tempered by "that firm and fixed ideal of American individualism—*an equality of opportunity*." Equality of opportunity, "the demand for a fair chance as the basis of American life": this was "our most precious social ideal." He insisted that equal opportunity and a "fair chance" for individuals to develop their abilities were "the sole source of progress" and the fundamental impulse behind American civilization for three centuries.

The secretary of commerce did not believe that equality of opportunity was automatically self-sustaining in a modern, industrial economy. A certain amount of governmental regulation and legislation (such as antitrust laws), he held, was necessary to prevent inequality of opportunity, private economic "autocracy," and the throttling of individual initiative. To Hoover, an orphaned son of an Iowa blacksmith, it was imperative that *"we keep the social solution free from frozen strata of classes."* The "human particles" (as he later put it) must be able to "move freely in the social solution." For him some governmental regulation was required to achieve that end.

Hoover, then, was no doctrinaire Social Darwinist. In *American Individualism* he explicitly repudiated laissez-faire, which he defined as "every man for himself and the devil take the hindmost." It was, he claimed, an outmoded social doctrine that America had abandoned "when we adopted the ideal of equality of opportunity—the fair chance of Abraham Lincoln."

At the same time, he emphatically rejected socialism and other statist ideologies. He denounced governmental operation of business as the "negation" of "our social foundations." In effect he was advocating a middle way of reform without revolution, avoiding the "equal dangers" of radicalism and reaction. Citing growing evidence of industrial self-regulation such as trade associations and cooperatives, he believed that a new era in American life was dawning: an era blending self-interest with the ethic of service and cooperation. In short, American individualism—"the most precious possession of American civilization"—was for him the still-valid formula for national progress.

Hoover's little book was no casual excursion into the realm of political philosophy. The publication of *American Individualism* in December 1922 had an immediate and very practical purpose. During the preceding months the United States had been beset by its most dangerous industrial strife since the 1890s. In April more than half a million coal miners had gone out on a nationwide strike. Less than three months later, 400,000 railroad workers had joined them. As the two strikes persisted through the summer, the nation's supply of coal for the coming winter plummeted and its transportation networks appeared headed for a total breakdown. In the words of the secretary of labor, America appeared to be "on the verge of industrial collapse."

Although the strikes were finally resolved by early autumn (Hoover was intimately involved in the episode), many Americans remained apprehensive. Once again social unrest of menacing proportions had reared its head. In the congressional elections that autumn, the Republican Party lost seventy seats in the House of Representatives. In the economically hard-pressed states in the American heartland, radical agrarians made notable gains.

Was a new outbreak of divisiveness and demagoguery brewing? Hoover appeared to fear that it was. Sometime in 1922 he evidently decided to convert his article on "American Individualism" into a book as an antidote to the impending political storm. Although the precise date of his decision is uncertain, within two days of the November election Hoover's staff took steps to rush his book into print. In an office memorandum on November 9, Hoover's assistant George Barr Baker explained the need for haste: immediate publication, he said, would "secure immediate dissemination of the ideas it contains" and leave Hoover "free to expand certain related material" in the spring. "With the public mind in its present state," Baker added, "and with the certainty that the next Congress will be very largely controlled by men with extreme views, of both parties, we recognize that the service this book can render must be immediate."[15]

Another Hoover intimate, Edgar Rickard, agreed. Appealing to no fewer than sixty friends to help in the book's distribution, he declared that *American Individualism* was "particularly needed" in "this time of unrest."[16] The book, he asserted, would "do much toward quieting the minds of people who are disturbed by present economic conditions."[17]

Throughout the rest of November, Hoover's aides labored to expedite the publishing process and lubricate the levers of publicity. On December 11, 1922, only five weeks after the election, *American Individualism* was published by Doubleday, Page & Co. Hoover's lieutenants and publisher promptly circulated his "sermon" (as Rickard called it) throughout the land.[18] Every newly elected member of Congress from the Middle West received a free copy, as did professors of economics in various colleges.[19] From Hoover's network of associates in his wartime public service came requests—encouraged by Rickard—for approximately 2,000 copies. By late January 1923, more than 9,600 copies had been sold outright, and the book had gone into its third printing.[20]

With the exception of the socialist press and the left-leaning *New Republic,* the response of reviewers to Hoover's tract was generally friendly.[21] In a lengthy analysis the *New York Times Book Review* predicted that, in content if not in style, *American Individualism* would rank "among the few great formulations of American political theory."[22] The book also found interested readers overseas. Eventually it was translated into German, Polish, Bulgarian, and Japanese.

Hoover's apotheosis of the United States as a nation dedicated to the ideal of equal opportunity evoked particular enthusiasm from the distinguished historian Frederick Jackson Turner, exponent of the influential "frontier thesis" as the key to understanding America's development. Hoover's "meaty little book," said Turner, "contains the New and the Old Testament of the American gospel and I wish it a wide circulation."[23] Interestingly, when Professor Turner's book *The Frontier in American History* had been published in 1920, he had given a copy to Hoover, who had read it (according to his secretary) "with very great interest."[24]

With the advent of prosperity in the mid-1920s, the searing labor conflicts and social upheavals of 1919–22 subsided, and the "Roaring Twenties" took hold. Whatever *American Individualism*'s contribution to this healing process may have been, Hoover's little "sermon" helped solidify his reputation as one of the ablest architects of what came to be called the New Era. Acclaimed as a "great humanitarian" and "master of emergencies," in 1928 he was elected president of the United States in a landslide—without ever having held an elective public office.

Looking back that year on the book he had published a half-decade before, Hoover told an acquaintance: "I am afraid the book is a little out of date as it was written when we were somewhat more exercised over socialistic and communistic movements than we need to be today."[25]

He could not foresee that his philosophy of

American individualism was about to face its starkest challenge.

II

What a difference a half-decade can make. In early 1928 Herbert Hoover was nearing the pinnacle of a spectacular public career. Five years later he was a former president, defeated overwhelmingly at the polls, his achievements and social philosophy seemingly repudiated forever by his own people.

During his tormented presidency (1929–33) Hoover struggled conscientiously against unending frustrations. As the greatest depression in American history lengthened and deepened, he exerted himself to the brink of exhaustion to return his country to prosperity and safeguard its traditional moorings. By the autumn of 1932 it appeared to the Republican president that these moorings were under dangerous assault from his left-wing political opponents. At the climax of the 1932 election campaign, in which he was seeking a second term, he portrayed the decision facing the American electorate as more than a choice between two men and two parties. It was a "contest between two philosophies of government," an election that would determine the nation's course for "over a century to come."[26] The American people did not heed his somber prophecies; he left office on March 4, 1933, a virtual pariah, despised and rejected like no other American in his lifetime.

At first the former president, ensconced in his home on the Stanford University campus, maintained public silence as the New Deal of his successor, Franklin Roosevelt, took shape. But as the months passed, Hoover's vexation and sense of foreboding became unbearable. To the earnest philosopher of American individualism, the unfolding New Deal was no mere spate of liberal reform or pragmatic response to economic distress. It was nothing less than a form of collectivism that, unchecked, would "destroy the very foundations of the American system of life."[27] In September 1933 he told a close friend: "The impending battle in this country obviously will be between a properly regulated individualism (which I have always expounded as 'American Individualism') and sheer socialism. That, directly or indirectly, is likely to be the great political battle for some years to come."[28]

Although Hoover continued to use the term "American Individualism" (and even considered reissuing his book of that title in 1933), increasingly he invoked another word, liberalism, to describe his embattled social philosophy.[29] Liberalism, he said late in 1933, "is an intangible, imponderable thing. It is the freedom of men's minds and spirits. It was born with the Renaissance, was re-enforced with the Reformation, was brought to reality by the American revolution, and has survived by much suffering down to the corruption of the great war [World War I]. Today we are engaged in creating regimented men, not free men, both in spirit and in economic life."[30]

For Hoover the fundamentals of historic liberalism were embodied in the United States Constitution, above all in the Bill of Rights. Increasingly in 1933–34, the Bill of Rights—that charter (in his words) of "ordered individual liberty"—was on his mind. "The discouraging thing," he lamented privately, "is that for some fancied economic boom the American people are prepared to sacrifice their most fundamental possession."[31] In America as well as Europe, the forces of illiberal statism appeared to be ascendant.

By early 1934 Hoover was at work on a book manuscript that would confront the statist ideologies on the terrain where he felt they must be fought: philosophy and principle. At first he titled his manuscript *American Liberalism*, recalling his initial foray into political theory a dozen years earlier.[32] But when his book was published in September 1934, it bore a more militant title: *The Challenge to Liberty*. According to Hoover the "American System" of liberty, a system infused by the philosophy of historic liberalism, was under siege. Where liberalism championed the individual as master of the state and possessor of inalienable rights, alternative philosophies were now boldly advocating "the idea of the servitude of the individual to the state." Among these noxious ideologies—all sharing this fundamental premise—were Nazism, socialism, fascism, communism, and "regimentation" (his term for Franklin Roosevelt's New Deal).

As in 1922, so now in 1934, Hoover freely conceded that the American regime of liberty had at times been abused. He carefully emphasized that America's traditional social philosophy was not one of unfettered laissez-faire. But he also insisted that the flaws in the pre–New Deal American system were "marginal," corrigible, and far less threatening to the nation than the "bureaucratic tyranny" that would accompany the collectivist alternatives. For Hoover the "false Liberalism" of the New Deal was the gateway to "dictation by government" and "the subjection of Liberty."

The Challenge to Liberty was Hoover's first major public statement since he had left the White House, and as he had anticipated, its appearance was an "event." Within days his book was a national best seller. By March 1935, just six months after its publication, more than 100,000 copies had been distributed.[33]

As in *American Individualism*, Hoover in *The Challenge to Liberty* sought to place himself in the political center. This time, no doubt to his disappointment, the attempt did not succeed. By 1934 the "middle ground" of American individualism was not holding. The nation was veering sharply to the left. Even the categories of political discourse were shifting their meaning, as Hoover came to acknowledge. In 1937 he confided to a friend: "The New Deal having corrupted the label of liberalism for collectivism, coercion [and] concentration of political power, it seems 'Historic Liberalism' must be conservatism in contrast."[34]

With these words of recognition Hoover's political odyssey was complete. The onetime Bull Moose Republican and self-styled "progressive" had become a man of the Right.

And so he remained for the rest of his very long life. The publication of *The Challenge to Liberty* marked Hoover's emergence from a year and a half of political exile. Crisscrossing the country in the mid- and late 1930s, he fired an unceasing barrage of verbal fusillades against New Deal statism and its defenders. In the process he became the Republican Party's intellectual leader and President Roosevelt's most formidable critic from the Right. Until his death in 1964 at the age of ninety, Hoover, the political philosopher and unflinching political prophet, relentlessly conducted what he called a "crusade against collectivism": a crusade that in some ways had its inception in the publication of *American Individualism* in 1922.

III

More than ninety years have passed since *American Individualism* was first published. It is clear, in retrospect, that the volume was in part motivated by the political controversies of the time.

Yet today, long after the circumstances that

INTRODUCTION

produced the book have disappeared, Hoover's
creed continues to invite our attention. Few American presidents have ventured self-consciously into
the realm of political philosophy; Hoover did. Unlike most American men of affairs, who have been
content to act on the public stage but not to medi-
tate much about it, he endeavored to explain the
essence of the American regime—a task that had
engaged observers like Alexis de Tocqueville and
Frederick Jackson Turner before him. This alone
gives the book lasting significance.

The importance of this tract, however, tran-
scends the scholarly concerns of historians and
social scientists, for *American Individualism* is not
simply a product of a dim and receding past. To
a considerable degree the ideological battles of
Hoover's era are the battles of our own, and the
interpretations we *make* of our past—particularly
the years between 1921 and 1933—mold our perspective on the crises of the present. To many of
those on the political Left, for instance, Franklin
Roosevelt's New Deal was essentially a moderate
reform movement that saved American capitalism from destruction and averted a revolution. To
Hoover and many on the Right, the New Deal *was*

a revolution that wrought a profound transformation in the relationship of government to citizen and of government to the economy—a transformation that would eventually stifle our liberties and poison the wellsprings of our prosperity. Nearly a century later the times are too perilous, and the portents of the future too ambiguous, to say with assurance that his prophecy was wrong.

There is a broader relevance still to the little volume before you. Of the forty-three individuals who have served as president of the United States, Herbert Hoover was more profoundly acquainted with foreign peoples and their social systems than were any of his predecessors or successors. Hoover's perception of contrast between the Old World and the New was the experiential core of his social and political philosophy and had an enduring effect upon him. It gave him a fervent sense of American uniqueness. To him the United States was "one of the last few strongholds of human freedom."

Today, as in Hoover's time, that stronghold is under challenge. Hoover labeled its core value system "American Individualism" and "Historic Liberalism." For us a comparable term, perhaps, would be "American Exceptionalism." But whatever the label, the reality is clear: over much of the Earth today, very different social and political philosophies are regnant, and many of their adherents have little sympathy for the American philosophy of ordered liberty that Hoover articulated.

In an era when defenders of "the American way of life" face daily assaults on our most precious ideals, *American Individualism* has more than passing interest. Hoover recognized that in a century of wars and revolutions it is philosophy, however perverted, that moves men and women for good or ill. It is imperative, therefore, that we comprehend our own. The book republished here can contribute to our national self-understanding.

This is no academic exercise. From a lifetime of comparative social analysis Herbert Hoover derived this lesson: in the destinies of nations, ideas—and ideals—have mattered.

They still do.

GEORGE H. NASH
South Hadley, Massachusetts
July 4, 2016

NOTES FOR THE INTRODUCTION

1. John Maynard Keynes, *The Economic Consequences of the Peace* (New York, 1920), p. 274n.
2. Herbert Hoover, "The Safety of New-born Democracies," *Forum* 62 (December 1919): 551.
3. Ibid., pp. 551, 560–61.
4. Ibid., p. 551.
5. Herbert Hoover, *The Memoirs of Herbert Hoover*, vol. I: *Years of Adventure* (New York, 1951), p. 473.
6. Ibid., p. 479.
7. Herbert Hoover, *The Challenge to Liberty* (New York, 1934), p. 38.
8. Herbert Hoover, inaugural address to the American Institute of Mining and Metallurgical Engineers (AIMME), February 17, 1920, Public Statements File, Herbert Hoover Papers, Herbert Hoover Presidential Library, West Branch, Iowa.
9. Hoover, "Safety of New-born Democracies," p. 561.

10. Ibid.

11. Hoover, inaugural address to AIMME, February 17, 1920.

12. Hoover, "Safety of New-born Democracies," p. 562.

13. Ibid., p. 561.

14. Mark Sullivan to Hoover, October 13, 1921, "*American Individualism*, 1921–1922," Commerce Papers, Hoover Papers; Hoover, "American Individualism," *World's Work* 43 (April 1922): 584–88. The caption under the title of Hoover's magazine article was revealing: "The Genius of Our Government and of Our Industry Reaffirmed Against Old World Philosophies and Experiments."

15. George Barr Baker memorandum, November 9, 1922, "*American Individualism*, 1922–1923 and Undated (5)," Commerce Papers.

16. Edgar Rickard, text of letter to his friends, n.d., ibid.

17. Edgar Rickard to Arthur Ryerson, December 20, 1922, "*American Individualism*, 1922–1923 and Undated (4)," Commerce Papers. See also Rickard to Howard J. Heinz, December 2, 1922, ibid.

18. Rickard to Heinz, December 2, 1922; various correspondence, 1922–23, passim, in the *American Individualism* files, Commerce Papers.

19. Arthur W. Page to Frank C. Page, January 24, 1923, "*American Individualism*, 1922–1923 and Undated (3)," Commerce Papers.

20. Rickard to J. F. Lucey, January 26, 1923, "*American Individualism*, 1922 1923 and Undated (4)," Commerce Papers.

21. See the two summaries of comment compiled by a member of Hoover's staff, February 9, and 21, 1923, "*American Individualism*, 1923 and Undated," Commerce Papers.

22. *New York Times Book Review,* December 17, 1922, p. 1.

23. Frederick Jackson Turner to Richard S. Emmet (a Hoover secretary), January 18, 1923, Commerce Papers.

24. Emmet to Turner, January 27, 1923, ibid.

25. Hoover to Homer Guck, May 8, 1928, "*American Individualism*, 1922–1923 and Undated, (1)," ibid.

26. Hoover speech in New York City, October 31, 1932; complete text in *Public Papers of the Presidents of the United States, Herbert Hoover: Containing the Public Messages, Speeches, and Statements of the President, January 1, 1932 to March 4, 1933* (Washington, DC, 1977), pp. 656–79.

27. Ibid., p. 657.

28. Hoover to Edward Eyre Hunt, September 14, 1933, Post-Presidential Individual (PPI) File, Hoover Papers.

29. Ibid.

30. Hoover to Will Irwin, December 16, 1933, PPI.

31. Hoover to Henry J. Allen, November 14, 1933, PPI.

32. Arch W. Shaw to Herbert Hoover, August 8, 1934, PPI.

33. H. Meier memorandum, March 22, 1935, "Books by HH: *The Challenge to Liberty*—Printing Arrangements," Post-Presidential Subject File, Hoover Papers.

34. Hoover to William Allen White, May 11, 1937, PPI.

AMERICAN
INDIVIDUALISM

AMERICAN
INDIVIDUALISM

We have witnessed in this last eight years the spread of revolution over one-third of the world. The causes of these explosions lie at far greater depths than the failure of governments in war. The war itself in its last stages was a conflict of social philosophies—but beyond this the causes of social explosion lay in the great inequalities and injustices of centuries flogged beyond endurance by the conflict and freed from restraint by the destruction of war. The urgent forces which drive human society have been plunged into a terrible furnace. Great theories spun by dreamers to remedy the pressing human ills have come to the front of men's minds. Great formulas came into life that promised to dissolve all trouble. Great masses of people have flocked to their banners in hopes born of misery and suffering. Nor has this great social ferment been confined to those nations that have burned with revolutions.

Now, as the storm of war, of revolution and of emotion subsides there is left even with us of the United States much unrest, much discontent with the surer forces of human advancement. To all of us, out of this crucible of actual, poignant, individual experience has come a deal of new understanding, and it is for all of us to ponder these new currents if we are to shape our future with intelligence.

Even those parts of the world that suffered less from the war have been partly infected by these ideas. Beyond this, however, many have had high hopes of civilization suddenly purified and ennobled by the sacrifices and services of the war; they had thought the fine unity of purpose gained in war would be carried into great unity of action in remedy of the faults of civilization in peace. But from concentration of every spiritual and material energy upon the single purpose of war the scene changed to the immense complexity and the many purposes of peace.

Thus there loom up certain definite underlying forces in our national life that need to be stripped of the imaginary—the transitory—and a definition should be given to the actual permanent and persistent motivation of our civilization. In contemplation of these questions we must go far deeper than the superficials of our political and economic structure, for these are but the products of our social philosophy—the machinery of our social system.

Nor is it ever amiss to review the political, economic, and spiritual principles through which our country has steadily grown in usefulness and greatness, not only to preserve them from being fouled by false notions, but more importantly that we may guide ourselves in the road of progress.

Five or six great social philosophies are at struggle in the world for ascendency. There is the Individualism of America. There is the Individualism of the more democratic states of Europe with its careful reservations of castes and classes. There are Communism, Socialism, Syndicalism, Capitalism, and finally there is Autocracy—whether by birth, by possessions, militarism, or divine right of kings. Even the Divine Right still lingers on although our lifetime has seen fully two-thirds of the earth's population, including Germany, Austria, Russia, and China, arrive at a state of angry disgust with this type of social motive power and throw it on the scrap heap.

All these thoughts are in ferment today in every country in the world. They fluctuate in ascendency with times and places. They compromise with each other in daily reaction on governments and peoples. Some of these ideas are perhaps more adapted to one race than another. Some are false, some are true. What we are interested in is their challenge to the physical and spiritual forces of America.

The partisans of some of these other brands of social schemes challenge us to comparison; and some of their partisans even among our own people are increasing in their agitation that we adopt one or another or parts of their devices in place of our tried individualism. They insist that our social foundations are exhausted, that like feudalism and autocracy America's plan has served its purpose— that it must be abandoned.

There are those who have been left in sober doubt of our institutions or are confounded by bewildering catchwords of vivid phrases. For in this welter of discussions there is much attempt to glorify or defame social and economic forces with phrases. Nor indeed should we disregard the potency of some of these phrases in their stir to action.—"The dictatorship of the Proletariat," "Capitalistic nations," "Germany over all," and a score of others. We need only to review those that have jumped to horseback during the last ten years in order that we may be properly awed by the great social and political havoc that can be worked where the bestial instincts of hate, murder, and destruction are clothed by the demagogue in the fine terms of political idealism.

For myself, let me say at the very outset that my faith in the essential truth, strength, and vitality of the developing creed by which we have hitherto lived in this country of ours has been confirmed and deepened by the searching experiences of seven years of service in the backwash and misery of war. Seven years of contending with economic degeneration, with social disintegration, with incessant political dislocation, with all of its seething and ferment of individual and class conflict, could but impress me with the primary motivation of social forces, and the necessity for broader thought upon their great issues to humanity. And from it all I emerge an individualist—an unashamed individualist. But let me say also that I am an American individualist. For America has been steadily developing the ideals that constitute progressive individualism.

No doubt, individualism run riot, with no tempering principle, would provide a long category of inequalities, of tyrannies, dominations, and injustices. America, however, has tempered the whole conception of individualism by the injection of a definite principle, and from this principle it follows that attempts at domination, whether in government or in the processes of industry and commerce, are under an insistent curb. If we would have the values of individualism, their stimulation to initiative, to the development of hand and intellect, to the high development of thought and spirituality, they must be tempered with that firm and fixed ideal of American individualism—*an equality of opportunity.* If we would have these values we must soften its hardness and stimulate progress through that sense of service that lies in our people.

Therefore, it is not the individualism of other countries for which I would speak, but the individualism of America. Our individualism differs from all others because it embraces these great ideals: *that while we build our society upon the attainment of the individual, we shall safeguard to every individual an equality of opportunity to take that position in the community to which his intelligence, character, ability, and ambition entitle him; that we keep the social solution free from frozen strata of classes; that we shall stimulate effort of each individual to achievement;*

that through an enlarging sense of responsibility and understanding we shall assist him to this attainment; while he in turn must stand up to the emery wheel of competition.

Individualism cannot be maintained as the foundation of a society if it looks to only legalistic justice based upon contracts, property, and political equality. Such legalistic safeguards are themselves not enough. In our individualism we have long since abandoned the laissez faire of the 18th Century—the notion that it is "every man for himself and the devil take the hindmost." We abandoned that when we adopted the ideal of equality of opportunity—the fair chance of Abraham Lincoln. We have confirmed its abandonment in terms of legislation, of social and economic justice,—in part because we have learned that it is the hindmost who throws the bricks at our social edifice, in part because we have learned that the foremost are not always the best nor the hindmost the worst— and in part because we have learned that social injustice is the destruction of justice itself. We have learned that the impulse to production can only be maintained at a high pitch if there is a fair division of the product. We have also learned that fair division can only be obtained by certain restrictions on the strong and the dominant. We have indeed gone even further in the 20th Century with the embracement of the necessity of a greater and broader sense of service and responsibility to others as a part of individualism.

Whatever may be the case with regard to Old World individualism (and we have given more back to Europe than we received from her) the truth that is important for us to grasp today is that there is a world of difference between the principles and spirit of Old World individualism and that which we have developed in our own country.

We have, in fact, a special social system of our own. We have made it ourselves from materials brought in revolt from conditions in Europe. We have lived it; we constantly improve it; we have seldom tried to define it. It abhors autocracy and does not argue with it, but fights it. It is not capitalism, or socialism, or syndicalism, nor a cross breed of them. Like most Americans, I refuse to be damned by anybody's word-classification of it, such as "capitalism," "plutocracy," "proletariat" or "middle class," or any other, or to any kind of compartment that is based on the assumption of some group dominating somebody else.

The social force in which I am interested is far higher and far more precious a thing than all these. It springs from something infinitely more enduring; it springs from the one source of human progress—that each individual shall be given the chance and stimulation for development of the best with which he has been endowed in heart and mind; it is the sole source of progress; it is American individualism.

The rightfulness of our individualism can rest either on philosophic, political, economic, or spiritual grounds. It can rest on the ground of being the only safe avenue to further human progress.

PHILOSOPHIC
GROUNDS

On the philosophic side we can agree at once
that intelligence, character, courage, and the divine
spark of the human soul are alone the property of
individuals. These do not lie in agreements, in organizations, in institutions, in masses, or in groups.
They abide alone in the individual mind and heart.

Production both of mind and hand rests upon
impulses in each individual. These impulses are
made of the varied forces of original instincts, mo-
tives, and acquired desires. Many of these are de-

structive and must be restrained through moral leadership and authority of the law and be eliminated finally by education. All are modified by a vast fund of experience and a vast plant and equipment of civilization which we pass on with increments to each succeeding generation.

The inherited instincts of self-preservation, acquisitiveness, fear, kindness, hate, curiosity, desire for self-expression, for power, for adulation, that we carry over from a thousand of generations must, for good or evil, be comprehended in a workable system embracing our accumulation of experiences and equipment. They may modify themselves with time—but in terms of generations. They differ in their urge upon different individuals. The dominant ones are selfish. But no civilization could be built or can endure solely upon the groundwork of unrestrained and unintelligent self-interest. The problem of the world is to restrain the destructive instincts while strengthening and enlarging those of altruistic character and constructive impulse— for thus we build for the future.

From the instincts of kindness, pity, fealty to family and race; the love of liberty; the mystical yearnings for spiritual things; the desire for fuller expression of the creative faculties; the impulses of service to community and nation, are moulded the ideals of our people. And the most potent force in society is its ideals. If one were to attempt to delimit the potency of instinct and ideals, it would be found that while instinct dominates in our preservation yet the great propelling force of progress is right ideals. It is true we do not realize the ideal; not even a single person personifies that realization. It is therefore not surprising that society, a collection of persons, a necessary maze of compromises, cannot realize it. But that it has ideals, that they revolve in a system that makes for steady advance of them is the first thing. Yet true as this is, the day has not arrived when any economic or social system will function and last if founded upon altruism alone.

With the growth of ideals through education, with the higher realization of freedom, of justice, of humanity, of service, the selfish impulses become less and less dominant, and if we ever reach the millennium, they will disappear in the aspirations and satisfactions of pure altruism. But for the next several generations we dare not abandon self-interest as a motive force to leadership and to production, lest we die.

The will-o'-the-wisp of all breeds of socialism is that they contemplate a motivation of human animals by altruism alone. It necessitates a bureaucracy of the entire population, in which, having obliterated the economic stimulation of each member, the fine gradations of character and ability are to be arranged in relative authority by ballot or more likely by a Tammany Hall or a Bolshevist party, or some other form of tyranny. The proof of the futility of these ideas as a stimulation to the development and activity of the individual does not lie alone in the ghastly failure of Russia, but it also lies in our own failure in attempts at nationalized industry.

Likewise the basic foundations of autocracy, whether it be class government or capitalism in the sense that a few men through unrestrained control of property determine the welfare of great numbers, is as far apart from the rightful expression of American individualism as the two poles. The will-o'-the-wisp of autocracy in any form is that it supposes that the good Lord endowed a special few with all the divine attributes. It contemplates one human animal dealing to the other human animals his just share of earth, of glory, and of immortality. The proof of the futility of these ideas in the development of the world does not lie alone in the grim failure of Germany, but it lies in the damage to our moral and social fabric from those who have sought economic domination in America, whether employer or employee.

We in America have had too much experience of life to fool ourselves into pretending that all men are equal in ability, in character, in intelligence, in ambition. That was part of the clap-trap of the French Revolution. We have grown to understand that all we can hope to assure to the individual through government is liberty, justice, intellectual welfare, equality of opportunity, and stimulation to service.

It is in maintenance of a society fluid to these human qualities that our individualism departs from the individualism of Europe. There can be no rise for the individual through the frozen strata of classes, or of castes, and no stratification can take place in a mass livened by the free stir of its particles. This guarding of our individualism against stratification insists not only in preserving in the social solution an equal opportunity for the able and ambitious to rise from the bottom; it also insists that the sons of the successful shall not by any mere right of birth or favor continue to occupy their fathers' places of power against the rise of a new generation in process of coming up from the bottom. The pioneers of our American individualism had the good sense not to reward Washington and Jefferson and Hamilton with hereditary dukedoms and fixtures in landed estates, as Great Britain rewarded Marlborough and Nelson. Otherwise our American fields of opportunity would have been clogged with long generations inheriting their fathers' privileges without their fathers' capacity for service.

That our system has avoided the establishment and domination of class has a significant proof in the present Administration in Washington. Of the twelve men comprising the President, Vice-President, and Cabinet, nine have earned their own way in life without economic inheritance, and eight of them started with manual labor.

If we examine the impulses that carry us forward, none is so potent for progress as the yearning for individual self-expression, the desire for creation of something. Perhaps the greatest human happiness flows from personal achievement. Here lies the great urge of the constructive instinct of mankind. But it can only thrive in a society where the individual has liberty and stimulation to achievement. Nor does the community progress except through its participation in these multitudes of achievements.

Furthermore, the maintenance of productivity and the advancement of the things of the spirit depend upon the ever-renewed supply from the mass of those who can rise to leadership. Our social, economic, and intellectual progress is almost solely dependent upon the creative minds of those individuals with imaginative and administrative intelligence who create or who carry discoveries to widespread application. No race possesses more than a small percentage of these minds in a single generation. But little thought has ever been given to our racial dependency upon them. Nor that our progress is in so large a measure due to the fact that with our increased means of communication these rare individuals are today able to spread their influence over so enlarged a number of lesser capable minds as to have increased their potency a million-fold. In truth, the vastly greater productivity of the world with actually less physical labor is due to the wider spread of their influence through the discovery of these facilities. And they can arise solely through the selection that comes from the free-running mills of competition. They must be free to rise from the mass; they must be given the attraction of premiums to effort.

Leadership is a quality of the individual. It is the individual alone who can function in the world of intellect and in the field of leadership. If democracy is to secure its authorities in morals, religion, and statesmanship, it must stimulate leadership from its own mass. Human leadership cannot be replenished by selection like queen bees, by divine right or bureaucracies, but by the free rise of ability, character, and intelligence.

Even so, leadership cannot, no matter how brilliant, carry progress far ahead of the average of the mass of individual units. Progress of the nation is the sum of progress in its individuals. Acts and ideas that lead to progress are born out of the womb of the individual mind, not out of the mind of the crowd. The crowd only feels: it has no mind of its own which can plan. The crowd is credulous, it destroys, it consumes, it hates, and it dreams—but it never builds. It is one of the most profound and important of exact psychological truths that man in the mass does not think but only feels. The mob functions only in a world of emotion. The demagogue feeds on mob emotions and his leadership is the leadership of emotion, not the leadership of intellect and progress. Popular desires are no criteria to the real need; they can be determined only by deliberative consideration, by education, by constructive leadership.

SPIRITUAL
PHASES

Our social and economic system cannot march toward better days unless it is inspired by things of the spirit. It is here that the higher purposes of individualism must find their sustenance. Men do not live by bread alone. Nor is individualism merely a stimulus to production and the road to liberty; it alone admits the universal divine inspiration of every human soul. I may repeat that the divine spark does not lie in agreements, in organizations, in institutions, in masses or in groups. Spirituality with its faith, its hope, its charity, can be increased by each individual's own effort. And in proportion as each individual increases his own store of spirituality, in that proportion increases the idealism of democracy.

For centuries, the human race believed that divine inspiration rested in a few. The result was blind faith in religious hierarchies, the Divine Right of Kings. The world has been disillusioned of this belief that divinity rests in any special group or class whether it be through a creed, a tyranny of kings or of proletariat. Our individualism insists upon the divine in each human being. It rests upon the firm faith that the divine spark can be awakened in every heart. It was the refusal to compromise these things that led to the migration of those religious groups who so largely composed our forefathers. Our diversified religious faiths are the apotheosis of spiritual individualism.

The vast multiplication of voluntary organizations for altruistic purposes are themselves proof of the ferment of spirituality, service, and mutual responsibility. These associations for advancement of public welfare, improvement, morals, charity, public opinion, health, the clubs and societies for recreation and intellectual advancement, represent something moving at a far greater depth than "joining." They represent the widespread aspiration for mutual advancement, self-expression, and neighborly helpfulness. Moreover, today when we rehearse our own individual memories of success, we find that none gives us such comfort as memory of service given. Do we not refer to our veterans as service men? Do not our merchants and business men pride themselves in something of service given beyond the price of their goods? When we traverse the glorious deeds of our fathers, we today never enumerate those acts that were not rooted in the soil of service. Those whom we revere are those who triumphed in service, for from them comes the uplift of the human heart and the uplift of the human mind.

While there are forces in the growth of our individualism which must be curbed with vigilance, yet there are no less glorious spiritual forces growing within that promise for the future. There is developing in our people a new valuation of individuals and of groups and of nations. It is a rising vision of service. Indeed if I were to select the social force that above all others has advanced sharply during these past years of suffering, it is that of service—service to those with whom we come in contact, service to the nation, and service to the world itself. If we examine the great mystical forces of the past seven years we find this great spiritual force poured out by our people as never before in the history of the world—the ideal of service.

Just now we are weakened by the feeling of failure of immediate realization of the great ideas and hopes that arose through the exaltation of war. War by its very nature sets loose chaotic forces of which the resultants cannot be foretold or anticipated. The insensitiveness to the brutalities of physical violence, and all the spiritual dislocations of war, have left us, at the moment, poorer. The amount of serenity and content in the world is smaller.

The spiritual reaction after the war has been in part the fruit of some illusions during those five years. In the presence of unity of purpose and the mystic emotions of war, many men came to believe that salvation lay in mass and group action. They have seen the spiritual and material mobilization of nations, of classes, and groups, for sacrifice and service; they have conceived that real human progress can be achieved by working on "the psychology of the people"—by the "mass mind"; they yielded to leadership without reservation; they conceived that this leadership could continue without tyranny; they have forgotten that permanent spiritual progress lies with the individual.

ECONOMIC
PHASES

That high and increasing standards of living and comfort should be the first of considerations in public mind and in government needs no apology. We have long since realized that the basis of an advancing civilization must be a high and growing standard of living for all the people, not for a single class; that education, food, clothing, housing, and the spreading use of what we so often term non-essentials, are the real fertilizers of the soil from which spring the finer flowers of life.

The economic development of the past fifty years has lifted the general standard of comfort far beyond the dreams of our forefathers. The only road to further advance in the standard of living is by greater invention, greater elimination of waste, greater production and better distribution of commodities and services, for by increasing their ratio to our numbers and dividing them justly we each will have more of them.

The superlative value of individualism through its impulse to production, its stimulation to invention, has, so far as I know, never been denied. Criticism of it has lain in its wastes but more importantly in its failures of equitable sharing of the product. In our country these contentions are mainly over the division to each of his share of the comforts and luxuries, for none of us is either hungry or cold or without a place to lay his head—and we have much besides. In less than four decades we have added electric lights, plumbing, telephones, gramophones, automobiles, and what not in wide diffusion to our standards of living. Each in turn began as a luxury, each in turn has become so commonplace that seventy or eighty per cent. of our people participate in them.

To all practical souls there is little use in quarreling over the share of each of us until we have something to divide. So long as we maintain our individualism we will have increasing quantities to share and we shall have time and leisure and taxes with which to fight out proper sharing of the "surplus." The income tax returns show that this surplus is a minor part of our total production after taxes are paid. Some of this "surplus" must be set aside for rewards to saving for stimulation of proper effort to skill, to leadership and invention— therefore the dispute is in reality over much less than the total of such "surplus." While there should be no minimizing of a certain fringe of injustices in sharing the results of production or in the wasteful use made by some of their share, yet there is vastly wider field for gains to all of us through cheapening the costs of production and distribution through the eliminating of their wastes, from increasing the volume of product by each and every one doing his utmost, than will ever come to us even if we can think out a method of abstract justice in sharing which did not stifle production of the total product.

It is a certainty we are confronted with a population in such numbers as can only exist by production attuned to a pitch in which the slightest reduction of the impulse to produce will at once create misery and want. If we throttle the fundamental impulses of man our production will decay. The world in this hour is witnessing the most overshadowing tragedy of ten centuries in the heartbreaking life-and-death struggle with starvation by a nation with a hundred and fifty millions of people. In Russia under the new tyranny a group, in pursuit of social theories, have destroyed the primary self-interest impulse of the individual to production.

Although socialism in a nation-wide application has now proved itself with rivers of blood and inconceivable misery to be an economic and spiritual fallacy and has wrecked itself finally upon the rocks of destroyed production and moral degeneracy, I believe it to have been necessary for the world to have had this demonstration. Great theoretic and emotional ideas have arisen before in the world's history and have in more than mere material bankruptcy deluged the world with fearful losses of life. A purely philosophical view might be that in the long run humanity has to try every way, even precipices, in finding the road to betterment.

But those are utterly wrong who say that individualism has as its only end the acquisition and preservation of private property—the selfish snatching and hoarding of the common product. Our American individualism, indeed, is only in part an economic creed. It aims to provide opportunity for self-expression, not merely economically, but spiritually as well. Private property is not a fetich in America. The crushing of the liquor trade without a cent of compensation, with scarcely even a discussion of it, does not bear out the notion that we give property rights any headway over human rights. Our development of individualism shows an increasing tendency to regard right of property not as an object in itself, but in the light of a useful and necessary instrument in stimulation of initiative to the individual; not only stimulation to him that he may gain personal comfort, security in life, protection to his family, but also because individual accumulation and ownership is a basis of selection to leadership in administration of the tools of industry and commerce. It is where dominant private property is assembled in the hands of the groups who control the state that the individual begins to feel capital as an oppressor. Our American demand for equality of opportunity is a constant militant check upon capital becoming a thing to be feared. Out of fear we sometimes even go too far and stifle the reproductive use of capital by crushing the initiative that makes for its creation.

Some discussion of the legal limitations we have placed upon economic domination is given later on, but it is desirable to mention here certain potent forces in our economic life that are themselves providing their own correction to domination.

The domination by arbitrary individual ownership is disappearing because the works of today are steadily growing more and more beyond the resources of any one individual, and steadily taxation will reduce relatively excessive individual accumulations. The number of persons in partnership through division of ownership among many stockholders is steadily increasing—thus 100,000 to 200,000 partners in a single concern are not uncommon. The overwhelmingly largest portion of our mobile capital is that of our banks, insurance companies, building and loan associations, and the vast majority of all this is the aggregated small savings of our people. Thus large capital is steadily becoming more and more a mobilization of the savings of the small holder—the actual people themselves—and its administration becomes at once more sensitive to the moral opinions of the people in order to attract their support. The directors and managers of large concerns, themselves employees of these great groups of individual stockholders, or policy holders, reflect a spirit of community responsibility.

Large masses of capital can only find their market for service or production to great numbers of the same kind of people that they employ and they must therefore maintain confidence in their public responsibilities in order to retain their customers. In times when the products of manufacture were mostly luxuries to the average of the people, the condition of their employees was of no such interest to their customers as when they cater to employees in general. Of this latter, no greater proofs need exist than the efforts of many large concerns directly dependent upon public good will to restrain prices in scarcity—and the very general desire to yield a measure of service with the goods sold. Another phase of this same development in administration of capital is the growth of a sort of institutional sense in many large business enterprises. The encouragement of solidarity in all grades of their employees in the common service and common success, the sense of mutuality with the prosperity of the community are both vital developments in individualism.

There has been in the last thirty years an extraordinary growth of organizations for advancement of ideas in the community for mutual coöperation and economic objectives—the chambers of commerce, trade associations, labor unions, bankers, farmers, propaganda associations, and what not. These are indeed variable mixtures of altruism and self-interest. Nevertheless, in these groups the individual finds an opportunity for self-expression and participation in the moulding of ideas, a field for training and the stepping stones for leadership.

The number of leaders in local and national life whose opportunity to service and leadership came through these associations has become now of more importance than those through the direct lines of political and religious organization.

At times these groups come into sharp conflict and often enough charge each other with crimes against public interest. They do contain faults; if they develop into warring interests, if they dominate legislators and intimidate public officials, if they are to be a new setting of tyranny, then they will destroy the foundation of individualism. Our Government will then drift into the hands of timorous mediocrities dominated by groups until we shall become a syndicalist nation on a gigantic scale. On the other hand, each group is a realization of greater mutuality of interest, each contains some element of public service and each is a school of public responsibility. In the main, the same forces that permeate the nation at large eventually permeate these groups. The sense of service, a growing sense of responsibility, and the sense of constructive opposition to domination, constantly recall in them their responsibilities as well as their privileges. In the end, no group can dominate the nation and a few successes in imposing the will of any group is its sure death warrant.

Today business organization is moving strongly toward coöperation. There are in the coöperative great hopes that we can even gain in individuality, equality of opportunity, and an enlarged field for initiative, and at the same time reduce many of the great wastes of overreckless competition in production and distribution. Those who either congratulate themselves or those who fear that coöperation is an advance toward socialism need neither rejoice or worry. Coöperation in its current economic sense represents the initiative of self-interest blended with a sense of service, for nobody belongs to a cooperative who is not striving to sell his products or services for more or striving to buy from others for less or striving to make his income more secure. Their members are furnishing the capital for extension of their activities just as effectively as if they did it in corporate form and they are simply transferring the profit principle from joint return to individual return. Their only success lies where they eliminate waste either in production or distribution—and they can do neither if they destroy individual initiative. Indeed this phase of development of our individualism promises to become the dominant note of its 20th Century expansion. But it will thrive only in so far as it can construct leadership and a sense of service, and so long as it preserves the initiative and safeguards the individuality of its members.

The economic system which is the result of our individualism is not a frozen organism. It moves rapidly in its form of organization under the impulse of initiative of our citizens, of growing science, of larger production, and of constantly cheapening distribution.

A great test of the soundness of a social system must be its ability to evolve within itself those orderly shifts in its administration that enable it to apply the new tools of social, economic, and intellectual progress, and to eliminate the malign forces that may grow in the application of these tools. When we were almost wholly an agricultural people our form of organization and administration, both in the governmental and economic fields, could be simple. With the enormous shift in growth to industry and commerce we have erected organisms that each generation has denounced as Frankensteins, yet the succeeding generation proves them to be controllable and useful. The growth of corporate organizations, of our banking systems, of our railways, of our electrical power, of our farm coöperatives, of our trade unions, of our trade associations, and of a hundred others indeed develops both beneficent and malign forces. The timid become frightened. But our basic social ideas march through the new things in the end. Our demagogues, of both radical and standpat breed, thrive on demands for the destruction of one or another of these organizations as the only solution for their defects, yet progress requires only a guardianship of the vital principles of our individualism with its safeguard of true equality of opportunity in them.

POLITICAL
PHASES

It is not the primary purpose of this essay to discuss our political organization. Democracy is merely the mechanism which individualism invented as a device that would carry on the necessary political work of its social organization. Democracy arises out of individualism and prospers through it alone.

Without question, there exists, almost all over the world, unprecedented disquietude at the functioning of government itself. It is in part the dreamy social ferment of war emotion. It is in part the aftermath of a period when the Government was everything and the individual nothing, from which there is much stimulation to two schools of thought: one that all human ills can be cured by governmental regulation, and the other that all regulation is a sin.

During the war, the mobilization of every effort, the destruction of the normal demand and the normal avenues of distribution, required a vast excursion over the deadline of individualism in order that we might secure immediate results. Its continuation would have destroyed the initiative of our people and undermined all real progress. We are slowly getting back, but many still aspire to these supposed short cuts to the millennium.

Much of our discontent takes the form of resentment against the inequalities in the distribution of the sacrifices of war. Both silently and vocally there is complaint that while some died, others ran no risk, and yet others profited. For these complaints there is adequate justification. The facts are patent. However, no conceivable human intelligence would be able to manage the conduct of war so as to see that all sacrifices and burdens should be distributed equitably. War is destruction, and we should blame war for its injustices, not a social system whose object is construction. The submergence of the individual, however, in the struggle of the race could be but temporary—its continuance through the crushing of individual action and its inequities would, if for no other reason, destroy the foundations of our civilization.

Looked at as the umpire in our social system, our Government has maintained an equality before the law and a development of legal justice and an authority in restraint of evil instincts that support this social system and its ideals so far as the imperfections of developing human institutions permit. It has gone the greatest distance of any government toward maintaining an equality of franchise; an equality of entrance to public office, and government by the majority. It has succeeded far beyond all others in those safeguards of equality of opportunity through education, public information, and the open channels of free speech and free press. It is, however, much easier to chart the course of progress to government in dealing with the abstract problems of order, political liberty, and stimulation to intellectual and moral advancement than it is to chart its relations to the economic seas. These seas are new and only partly discovered or explored.

Our Government's greatest troubles and failures are in the economic field. Forty years ago the contact of the individual with the Government had its largest expression in the sheriff or policeman, and in debates over political equality. In those happy days the Government offered but small interference with the economic life of the citizen. But with the vast development of industry and the train of regulating functions of the national and municipal government that followed from it; with the recent vast increase in taxation due to the war;—the Government has become through its relations to economic life the most potent force for maintenance or destruction of our American individualism.

The entrance of the Government began strongly three decades ago, when our industrial organization began to move powerfully in the direction of consolidation of enterprise. We found in the course of this development that equality of opportunity and its corollary, individual initiative, was being throttled by the concentration of control of industry and service, and thus an economic domination of groups builded over the nation. At this time, particularly, we were threatened with a form of autocracy of economic power. Our mass of regulation of public utilities and our legislation against restraint of trade is the monument to our intent to preserve an equality of opportunity. This regulation is itself proof that we have gone a long way toward the abandonment of the "capitalism" of Adam Smith.

Day by day we learn more as to the practical application of restrictions against economic and political domination. We sometimes lag behind in the correction of those forces that would override liberty, justice, and equality of opportunity, but the principle is so strong within us that domination of the few will not be tolerated. These restraints must keep pace with the growing complexity of our economic organization, but they need tuning to our social system if they would not take us into great dangers. As we build up our powers of production through the advancing application of science we create new forces with which men may dominate—railway, power, oil, and what not. They may produce temporary blockades upon equality of opportunity.

To curb the forces in business which would destroy equality of opportunity and yet to maintain the initiative and creative faculties of our people are the twin objects we must attain. To preserve the former we must regulate that type of activity that would dominate. To preserve the latter, the Government must keep out of production and distribution of commodities and services. This is the deadline between our system and socialism. Regulation to prevent domination and unfair practices, yet preserving rightful initiative, are in keeping with our social foundations. Nationalization of industry or business is their negation.

When we come to the practical problems of government in relation to these economic questions the test lies in two directions: Does this act safeguard an equality of opportunity? Does it maintain the initiative of our people? For in the first must lie the deadline against domination, and in the second the deadline in preservation of individualism against socialism. Excluding the temporary measures of the war, the period of regulation has now been long enough with us to begin to take stock of its effect upon our social system. It has been highly beneficial, but it has also developed weaknesses in the throttling of proper initiative that require some revision. We have already granted relief to labor organizations and to agriculture from some forms of regulation. There is, however, a large field of coöperative possibilities far outside agriculture that are needlessly hampered.

The most important of considerations in any attempt to pass judgment upon social systems is whether we maintain within them permanent and continuous motivation toward progress. These forces must be of two orders, one spiritual and the other economic.

We may discover the situation in our own social system either by an analysis of the forces that are today in motion or by noting the strides of progress over the century or over the last ten years. By a consideration of the forces that move us we can see whether our system shows signs of decay, whether its virility is maintained; and by the touchstone of time we can find out whether these forces have been powerful enough to overcome the malign influences that would lessen the well-being of our system.

If we should survey the fundamentals of our civilization from the point of view of its progress by the test of time, we can find much for satisfaction and assurance. It is unnecessary to recount the values of economic individualism in stimulation to invention; large constructive vision; intensity in production with decreased physical effort; our increased standards of living and comfort. It is of course easy to enumerate our great economic progress, but the progress of the social forces that will sustain economic progress is infinitely more important—for upon them depends the real future of our people. Education in its many phases has made much advance. The actual equipment, the character of instruction, the numbers reached, period of instruction—show improvement with every decade. Public opinion has become of steadily increasing potency and reliability in its reaction. The great strides in development of processes and equipment for production and distribution are being followed by increasing devotion to the human factors in their execution. Moral standards of business and commerce are improving; vicious city governments are less in number; invisible government has greatly diminished; public conscience is penetrating deeper and deeper; the rooting up of wrong grows more vigorous; the agencies for their exposure and remedy grow more numerous, and above all is the growing sense of service. Many people confuse the exposure of wrongs which were below the surface with degeneration; their very exposure is progress. Some accredit the exposures of failure in our government and business as evidence of standards of a lower order than in some other nations. A considerable experience leads me to the conviction that while we do wash our dirty linen in public most others never wash it.

It is easy to arraign any existing institution. Men can rightly be critical because things have happened that never ought to happen. That our social system contains faults no one disputes. One can recite the faulty results of our system at great length; the spirit of lawlessness; the uncertainty of employment in some callings; the deadening effect of certain repetitive processes of manufacture; the 12-hour day in a few industries; unequal voice in bargaining for wage in some employment; arrogant domination by some employers and some labor leaders; child labor in some states; inadequate instruction in some areas; unfair competition in some industries; some fortunes excessive far beyond the needs of stimulation to initiative; survivals of religious intolerance; political debauchery of some cities; weaknesses in our governmental structure. Most of these occur locally in certain regions and certain industries and must cause every thinking person to regret and to endeavor. But they are becoming steadily more local. That they are recognized and condemned is a long way on the road to progress.

One of the difficulties in social thought is to find the balance of perspective. A single crime does not mean a criminal community. It is easy to point out undernourished, overworked, uneducated children, children barred from the equality of opportunity that our ideals stand for. It is easy to point out the luxurious petted and spoiled children with favored opportunity in every community. But if we take the whole thirty-five millions of children of the United States, it would be a gross exaggeration to say that a million of them suffer from any of these injustices. This is indeed a million too many, but it is the thirty-four million that tests the system with the additional touchstone of whether there are forces in motivation which are insistently and carefully working for the amelioration of the one million. Its by-products of endowed loafers, or hoodlums, at respective ends of the economic scale, are indeed spectacular faults. Yet any analysis of the 105,000,000 of us would show that we harbor less than a million of either rich or impecunious loafers. If we measure our people by scales of other civilized peoples, we also find consolation. We have a distaste for the very expression of "class," but if we would use European scales of "classes" we would find that above their scale of "lower classes" we have in equivalent comfort, morality, understanding, and intelligence fully eighty per cent. of our native-born whites. No European state will lay claim to thirty per cent. of this order. Does this not mean that we have been gaining something?

I do not conceive that any man, or body of men, could ever be capable of drafting a plan that would solve these multiple difficulties in advance. Moreover, if we continue to advance we will find new difficulties and weaknesses as the by-product of progress—but to be overcome.

THE
FUTURE

Individualism has been the primary force of American civilization for three centuries. It is our sort of individualism that has supplied the motivation of America's political, economic, and spiritual institutions in all these years. It has proved its ability to develop its institutions with the changing scene. Our very form of government is the product of the individualism of our people, the demand for an equal opportunity, for a fair chance.

The American pioneer is the epic expression of that individualism, and the pioneer spirit is the response to the challenge of opportunity, to the challenge of nature, to the challenge of life, to the call of the frontier. That spirit need never die for lack of something for it to achieve. There will always be a frontier to conquer or to hold as long as men think, plan, and dare. Our American individualism has received much of its character from our contacts with the forces of nature on a new continent. It evolved government without official emissaries to show the way; it plowed and sowed two score of great states; it built roads, bridges, railways, cities; it carried forward every attribute of high civilization over a continent. The days of the pioneer are not over. There are continents of human welfare of which we have penetrated only the coastal plain. The great continent of science is as yet explored only on its borders, and it is only the pioneer who will penetrate the frontier in the quest for new worlds to conquer. The very genius of our institutions has been given to them by the pioneer spirit. Our individualism is rooted in our very nature. It is based on conviction born of experience. Equal opportunity, the demand for a fair chance, became the formula of American individualism because it is the method of American achievement.

After the absorption of the great plains of the

West came the era of industrial development with the new complex of forces that it has brought us. Now haltingly, but with more surety and precision than ever before and with a more conscious understanding of our mission, we are finding solution of these problems arising from new conditions, for the forces of our social system can compass and comprise these.

Our individualism is no middle ground between autocracy—whether of birth, economic or class origin—and socialism. Socialism of different varieties may have something to recommend it as an intellectual stop-look-and-listen sign, more especially for Old World societies. But it contains only destruction to the forces that make progress in our social system. Nor does salvation come by any device for concentration of power, whether political or economic, for both are equally reversions to Old World autocracy in new garments.

Salvation will not come to us out of the wreckage of individualism. What we need today is steady devotion to a better, brighter, broader individualism—an individualism that carries increasing responsibility and service to our fellows.

Our need is not for a way out but for a way forward. We found our way out three centuries ago when our forefathers left Europe for these shores, to set up here a commonwealth conceived in liberty and dedicated to the development of individuality.

There are malign social forces other than our failures that would destroy our progress. There are the equal dangers both of reaction and radicalism. The perpetual howl of radicalism is that it is the sole voice of liberalism—that devotion to social progress is its field alone. These men would assume that all reform and human advance must come through government. They have forgotten that progress must come from the steady lift of the individual and that the measure of national idealism and progress is the quality of idealism in the individual. The most trying support of radicalism comes from the timid or dishonest minds that shrink from facing the result of radicalism itself but are devoted to defense of radicalism as proof of a liberal mind. Most theorists who denounce our individualism as a social basis seem to have a passion for ignorance of its constructive ideals.

An even greater danger is the destructive criticism of minds too weak or too partisan to harbor constructive ideas. For such, criticism is based upon the distortion of perspective or cunning misrepresentation. There is never danger from the radical himself until the structure and confidence of society has been undermined by the enthronement of destructive criticism. Destructive criticism can certainly lead to revolution unless there are those willing to withstand the malice that flows in return from refutation. It has been well said that revolution is no summer thunderstorm clearing the atmosphere. In modern society it is a tornado leaving in its path the destroyed homes of millions with their dead women and children.

There are also those who insist that the future must be a repetition of the past; that ideas are dangerous, that ideals are freaks.

To find that fine balance which links the future with the past, whose vision is of men and not of tools, that possesses the courage to construct rather than to criticize—this is our need. There is no oratory so easy, no writing so trenchant and vivid as the phrase-making of criticism and malice—there is none so difficult as inspiration to construction.

We cannot ever afford to rest at ease in the comfortable assumption that right ideas always prevail by some virtue of their own. In the long run they do. But there can be and there have been periods of centuries when the world slumped back toward darkness merely because great masses of men became impregnated with wrong ideas and wrong social philosophies. The declines of civilization have been born of wrong ideas. Most of the wars of the world, including the recent one, have been fought by the advocates of contrasting ideas of social philosophy.

The primary safeguard of American individualism is an understanding of it; of faith that it is the most precious possession of American civilization, and a willingness courageously to test every process of national life upon the touchstone of this basic social premise. Development of the human institutions and of science and of industry have been long chains of trial and error. Our public relations to them and to other phases of our national life can be advanced in no other way than by a willingness to experiment in the remedy of our social faults. The failures and unsolved problems of economic and social life can be corrected; they can be solved within our social theme and under no other system. The solution is a matter of will to find solution; of a sense of duty as well as of a sense of right and citizenship. No one who buys "bootleg" whiskey can complain of gunmen and hoodlumism.

Humanity has a long road to perfection, but we of America can make sure progress if we will preserve our individualism, if we will preserve and stimulate the initiative of our people, if we will build up our insistence and safeguards to equality of opportunity, if we will glorify service as a part of our national character. Progress will march if we hold an abiding faith in the intelligence, the initiative, the character, the courage, and the divine touch in the individual. We can safeguard these ends if we give to each individual that opportunity for which the spirit of America stands. We can make a social system as perfect as our generation merits and one that will be received in gratitude by our children.

THE END

ABOUT THE AUTHORS

Herbert Hoover

(1874–1964)

Herbert Hoover was the 31st President of the United States, from 1929 to 1933. An internationally acclaimed humanitarian, Hoover was the author of more than thirty books and founder of the Hoover Institution on War, Revolution and Peace.

George H. Nash

A historian, lecturer, and authority on the life of Herbert Hoover, Nash's publications include three volumes of a definitive, scholarly biography of

Hoover and the monograph *Herbert Hoover and Stanford University*. He is the editor of two posthumously published memoirs by Herbert Hoover: *Freedom Betrayed* and *The Crusade Years*. Nash is also the author of *The Conservative Intellectual Movement in America Since 1945* and *Reappraising the Right: The Past and Future of American Conservatism*. A graduate of Amherst College and holder of a PhD in history from Harvard University, he received the Richard M. Weaver Prize for Scholarly Letters in 2008. He lives in South Hadley, Massachusetts.